SPECIAL READER BONUS

Get My Free 1-Hour Training

**How To Use A Short Book To
Generate 30+ Warm Leads
From LinkedIn Per Month**

When sorted by income 60% of LinkedIn users in the United States have an income of $100,000+.

41 percent of millionaires are on LinkedIn.

More than any other social network out there, the average user on LinkedIn is affluent. And where there's money, there are opportunities.

And as an exclusive and special gift for readers of *The Short Book Formula*, you'll get free access to this complementary must-have 1-hour video training.

Go to
www.theshortbookformula.com/bonus
to claim.

ALSO BY PAUL G. MCMANUS

Smart Million-Dollar Producer: The Secret Playbook For Financial Professionals To Land High-Value Clients Using LinkedIn

Million-Dollar Producer: The Secret Playbook For Financial Professionals To Land High-Value Clients Using LinkedIn

CO-AUTHORED BOOKS

The Due Diligence Project: How Open Source, Peer-Reviewed Due Diligence Is Supercharging Elite CPA Firms and Family Offices, While Disrupting a Trillion Dollar Industry

Wealth Beyond Taxes: How Pharmaceutical Professionals are Using the Tax Code to Their Advantage to Generate More Income and Wealth

The Short Book Formula

A Financial Professional's Guide to Writing a Book
in 6 Weeks to Attract Ideal Clients

Paul G. McManus

COPYRIGHT © 2023 by Paul G. McManus

All rights reserved. No part of this book may be used or reproduced in any manner whatsoever without prior written consent of the author, except as provided by the United States of America copyright law.

Published by MCMF Publishing

DISCLAIMER:

This book contains the opinions and ideas of the author. Careful attention has been paid to ensure the accuracy of the information, but the author cannot assume responsibility for the validity or consequences of its use. The material in this book is for informational purposes only. As each individual situation is unique, the author disclaims responsibility for any adverse effects that may result from the use or application of the information contained in this book. Any use of the information found in this book is the sole responsibility of the reader.

Contents

Part 1 - Welcome

Foreword - Liz Briggson..1
Who This Book Is For...5
My Promise To You...9
Introduction..13

Part 2 - The Short Book Formula

Chapter 1: Why Write A Book?....................................23
Chapter 2: The Secret to Engaging Your Reader..35
Chapter 3: The Short Book Formula.....................43
Chapter 4: Short Book Formula Examples............55
Chapter 5: Your Book As Your Business Card.......67
Chapter 6: The Value of a Book Launch Party......73
Chapter 7: How To Grow A 7-Figure Financial Practice...79

Part 3 – The Path Forward

Chapter 8: The Next Step.......................................91
Resources..95
About..97

Dedication

This book is dedicated to all of my amazing business mentors and collaborators.

Specifically, I'd like to thank my dad, Rick McManus, for all his help and support in running my company; Tony Maree Torrey for helping me over the past 8 years build a business that I love; Dan S. Kennedy for teaching me about authority marketing and the value of being a published author; and Mike Capuzzi, who inspired and taught me how to write my very first short book.

PART 1

WELCOME

FOREWORD

How would you feel to hold your very own published book in your hand? In this book you will learn from someone who has been there the very steps to follow to experience this accomplishment for yourself. While considering the end result of this achievement, take a moment to contemplate the process.

Putting a book out into the world involves reflection of what is most important to you and organization of the concepts that you believe are most impactful to your audience. The most difficult part is often stepping back and deciphering exactly who you want to reach with your message and what they most need to hear.

This is the hidden value in authoring a book that Paul McManus can best help with. In the most genuine way, Paul is skilled at asking the right questions and uncovering the pivotal elements that help people shine. I know this because I have worked with Paul for several years. I have had the privilege of hosting Paul on numerous webinars. He even interviewed me for his podcast at one point and it was one of the most comfortable and personable conversations I have had about the work that I do through Encoursa.

Paul combines his years of marketing experience, his genuine interest in getting to know people, and his expertise in utilizing the leading online platforms to bring about results for his clients. He is straightforward and motivating. Every time I talk to Paul, I learn a new marketing technique and I feel empowered to put it into action. The Encoursa audience consistently provides great feedback on Paul's instruction.

In The Short Book Formula, Paul lays out the exact path for building your authority with a book. You will learn not only how to uncover the needs your ideal clients are looking to meet, you will discover how to structure your solutions to create a compelling response to those needs. And Paul follows through to provide examples of how you can use your book in real life situations to open doors and win more of the work you are looking for.

As an author of three books, a frequent speaker to CPAs on the topic of building online presence, and the founder of More Clients More Fun, Paul is uniquely qualified to help financial professionals build their authority through writing a book.

After reading this book, you will want to start writing down your ideas and schedule time with Paul to bring your own book to life. We can all use someone in our corner to propel us to new heights.

Liz Briggson, CPA
Director of Education & Partnerships
Encoursa

Who This Book Is For

We both know time is precious, and I surely do not want to waste your time if *The Short Book Formula: A Financial Professional's Guide to Writing a Book in 6 Weeks to Attract Ideal Clients* is not for you. Therefore, let me be upfront and crystal clear on exactly who I wrote this book for.

I wrote *The Short Book Formula* for financial professionals - mainly financial advisors, tax-planning-focused CPAs, life insurance producers, and business advisors - who want to leverage the speed, control, and autonomy of being a self-published author. These men and women are skilled in financial planning, tax planning, exit planning, and other business advisory services. They play a crucial role in the success of business owners and high-net-worth individuals.

The *Short Book Formula* is for the financial professional who would like a quick and effective way to become a published author so that they can then get their book out into the world to help them attract their ideal clients.

I believe that writing and publishing a book should be a quick, efficient, and profitable process. That's why I have developed a unique approach that allows financial professionals to write and publish their books in record time, without sacrificing quality.

By following the methods in this book, you'll discover how to make it blindingly obvious to your ideal prospects that you are the only logical choice for them, and that you have a tremendous amount of value to bring to the table.

Our approach to writing and publishing is designed to help our authors create books that are focused, concise, and easy to understand. We believe that by using simple, clear language and avoiding unnecessary jargon or complexity we can help our authors create books that are accessible and enjoyable to read, even for those with limited time.

But the real value of our approach is in the way it connects your book to your products and services. By offering helpful information first, and then carefully connecting the dots to your offerings, you can make a lasting impression on your readers and entice them to want to do business with you.

And the best part? You don't have to rely on selling books to make money. Instead, our book-centric sales and marketing approach will help you target the right readers, have them raise their hands when the time is right, and help you easily convert them into paying clients.

So, if all this sounds good to you, please keep reading...

My Promise To You

This book exists for two reasons:

Reason #1: So that you'll eventually hire me and my team to help you implement everything you read here.

Reason #2: To inspire and motivate you on the benefits of writing and publishing a short book so that you'll actually want to do Reason #1 as quickly as possible.

The first thing I want you to know about me is that as a book coach, ghostwriter, and marketing expert, I have seen firsthand the transformative power of writing and publishing a book. Not only does it provide financial professionals with a powerful marketing tool that can help them attract more clients and grow their business, but it also helps them build credibility, authority, and influence in their field.

I have helped my clients navigate the often-intimidating world of publishing, providing them with the guidance, support, and resources they need to write, publish, and market their books successfully. And I am proud to say that many of my clients have seen great success, with some who have used their book to land speaking engagements, media interviews, and other high-profile opportunities.

The other thing I want you to know about me is that I am a Book Yourself Solid® Certified Coach, having been personally instructed in 2014 by Michael Port, author of the New York Times bestseller, *Book Yourself Solid: The Fastest, Easiest, and Most Reliable System for Getting More Clients Than You Can Handle Even If You Hate Marketing and Selling.*

Being a Book Yourself Solid® Certified Coach is important for you to know because it means that I have been trained by one of the foremost experts in the field of marketing and sales for service-based businesses. Since 2015 I have worked closely with over 500 financial professionals and business advisors to help them generate more leads, appointments, and sales by adopting a book-centric marketing approach to their business.

I share all this with you not to brag, but instead to let you know you are in good hands and that I know from years of experience how to help financial professionals grow their practice - oftentimes to 7-figures and beyond.

I promise to do my part and give you a proven and effective system that will help you become an author so you can attract your ideal clients.

Introduction

As a small business owner, I was always looking for ways to attract the right clients and charge the fees I felt I deserved. But with so much competition out there, especially online, it was tough to stand out and make myself known. That's when I decided to write my first book: Million Dollar Producer: The Secret Playbook For Financial Professionals To Land High-Value Clients Using LinkedIn back in 2019.

At first, I was intimidated by the thought of writing a whole book, but I was determined to make it happen. So, I started writing and before I knew it, I had a draft. And even though I hadn't finished the book yet, I decided to share the cover of it on social media.

The response was amazing. People congratulated me, and told me how

impressed they were. It felt great. And I hadn't even published it yet!

But the most important thing was once I did publish it, it quickly became an integral part of my marketing and sales process. Suddenly, I was no longer perceived as a salesperson - I was now an authority, an expert, a teacher. And that gave me the confidence and credibility to charge higher fees and attract the clients I wanted to work with.

How My First Book Helped Me Achieve A 80% Close Ratio

As we begin this journey together, I want you to understand that the type of book I am suggesting you write is first and foremost a sales tool for your business. I remember an incident shortly after I published my first book. A prospect named Tim had been referred to me for my services. In such cases, I typically agree to a 15-minute phone call to determine if the person is a good fit for my services and see if they are genuinely interested in what I have to offer. If the call goes well, we schedule a second appointment on Zoom.

One of the keys to this process of achieving an 80% close rate for me is giving my prospective clients a copy of my book and asking them to read it before the next meeting. Because the book can be read from cover to cover in under an hour, I feel that this is a reasonable request and a great way to determine how serious they are about wanting my help to solve their problem. If they refuse, I don't schedule the next call. This simple step ensures that I don't waste my time on tire kickers and allows me to focus on clients who are genuinely interested in my services. It has become an integral part of my sales process and has helped me avoid wasting time on unproductive meetings.

Tim agreed to both the reading assignment and to schedule the next Zoom call with me. When we met on Zoom the following Thursday, I asked him about his key takeaways from the book. To my surprise, he admitted that he had forgotten to read it. I felt a surge of frustration and let him know that because he didn't read the book, our meeting wouldn't be very productive.

"*I'm so sorry*," Tim said, his face on the Zoom screen flushed with embarrassment. "I can have the book read in the next few days. Can we reschedule?" I hesitated, not wanting to waste any more of my time. But something in Tim's sincere apology and genuine interest in my services made me agree to reschedule.

A few days later, we met again on Zoom. This time, Tim was able to discuss the book in detail and shared some of the key points that resonated with him. When I asked if he had any questions, he said he was very interested in moving forward with my services.

We discussed pricing and the next steps, and since then Tim has become one of my best clients. He has since referred me to many more clients.

Since then, interweaving my book with both my marketing and sales process has allowed me to achieve an 80% close rate. I've been able to avoid tire kickers, and those who are not serious about doing business with me. Even better, those who do become clients of mine tend to be ideal. They have a great appreciation for the work I do and are genuinely excited about my help. And best of all, because they value the work I do so much, they readily spread the word to their colleagues and others who would most benefit from my services, allowing me to spend very little money on advertising.

Is this your current experience with prospects?

If you're feeling frustrated with your current experience with prospects, I am thrilled that you have found your way to this book. I truly hope that the one hour you invest in carefully reading this book from cover to cover will provide you with a fresh perspective and renewed enthusiasm for not just increasing your revenue but building a financial practice filled with ideal clients who truly value your expertise and services.

It's time to take control of your business and create the success you deserve. With the insights and strategies shared in this book, you can learn to attract the right clients, charge higher fees, close larger cases, and earn the respect you deserve.

In conclusion, becoming a published author can have a powerful impact on both your own confidence and competence, as well as the way others perceive you. The added credibility and respect that comes with being an author can make all the difference in growing your business and achieving your goals. It's not just about the book itself but the sense of pride and accomplishment it brings to the author. As you embark on this journey of writing and publishing a book, remember the potential it holds to transform your life and business for the better.

So, get comfortable, grab a highlighter, pen, and paper, and get ready to join me for an enlightening journey. If you have any questions or comments, feel free to reach out to me at Paul@MoreClientsMoreFun.com

Enjoy the ride!
Paul

PART 2

THE SHORT BOOK FORMULA

Chapter 1

Why Write a Book?

According to a survey of 200 business owners, here were the key findings when it comes to the return on investment for authoring a book for one's business:

- 94% said it improved their brands
- 95% said it generated more speaking engagements
- 96% said it generated more clients
- 94% said it generated more leads
- 87% said it allowed them to charge higher fees
- 87% said it generated a more desirable client base
- 76% said it allowed them to close more deals

With such overwhelmingly positive results, the better question might be, why wouldn't a financial professional write a book? You are very likely an expert in your field with valuable insights and experiences to share. Writing a book can help establish your credibility, showcase your knowledge, and provide a new way to attract your ideal clients to you. However, as with any creative endeavor, writing a book comes with its own set of challenges.

Common Challenges Financial Professionals Face

- **Time:** Writing a book takes time, and it can be difficult to find the time to do it.
- **Content:** It can be challenging to come up with the right content for your book and to organize it in a way that will be useful and engaging for your readers.
- **Where to start:** It can seem overwhelming trying to figure out where to begin when writing a book, and it can be challenging to stay focused and organized throughout the process.
- **Publishing resources:** There are many options for publishing a book, and it can be difficult to know which one is right for you

and to find the right resources to help you with the process.
- **Confidence:** It can be intimidating to put yourself out there as an expert and to share your knowledge and experience with others. Imposter syndrome can make it hard to believe in your own expertise and to have the confidence to share it with the world.

The good news is that these are common concerns that many have. And throughout this book that you are reading now, we are going to provide you with solutions so that you can write and publish your own book in as little as six weeks.

Authorship and The Speed of Trust

Everyone understands the value of having a visible, respected corporate brand. But few understand the power of a personal brand. Most financial professionals launch a business and focus on building visibility or equity for the corporate logo and name, whether it be through high-end graphic design, expensive advertising campaigns, a dominant social media presence, or even PR.

When you focus on your corporate brand, you are not only playing a game everyone else is playing, you're often playing against some of the biggest brands in the world. When you go head-to-head with large established brands, you often find yourself in a losing battle because you're chasing a brand that has a several decades head start in terms of awareness, and often a marketing budget. This is a fool's errand, as you just don't have the resources or name recognition to compete with the biggest corporate brands in the industry.

Authorship levels the playing field by focusing on an individual's personal brand, meaning that you essentially become your own brand. Against that backdrop of a marketplace that is increasingly skeptical of large corporate brands, authorship can help accelerate the Speed of Trust like nothing else.

Imagine a business owner's company was just acquired for an eight-figure amount, and the owner, Bob, was interviewing four different financial professionals who specialize in exit planning and advanced tax strategies, and each of these professionals has the expertise and experience necessary to earn the business and provide sound financial advice.

Assuming each of the four financial professionals is trustworthy and has good relationship skills, what makes one stand out versus another, especially if each one is associated with large firms that have established brands? Not much, right?

Now imagine that one of our four financial professionals, Ryan, has published several short books on the topics of exit planning and advanced tax planning. Ryan is frequently quoted in the news. When Business Owner Bob does a Google search on Ryan's name, there are a plethora of links to his books, as well as well-known media sites. Bob orders copies of two of Ryan's books from Amazon and spends an hour reading each book from cover to cover.

Who do you think Bob The Business Owner chooses to hire?

Because Ryan had already established his credibility before Bob ever met him in person, instead of feeling like he's about to receive a sales pitch, Bob feels fortunate to have gotten a meeting with such an authority, and Ryan now has a significant edge as he's prescribing solutions instead of selling services.

Clients' Case Files: "From Commoditized CPA to Leading Authority: How Steve Used Authority Marketing to Stand Out in a Crowded Field"

As Steve reviewed his notes in the car on the way to the conference center, he couldn't help but feel a mix of excitement and nerves. He had been preparing for this moment for weeks, and now it was finally here. As the car pulled up to the building, Steve took a deep breath and steeled himself for the task ahead. He was about to appear on stage to speak to a group of affluent dentists, and he was determined not to let nerves get the best of him.

Just a few years ago, Steve was a typical CPA engaged in tax preparation for clients. waiting for his next client meeting. Now, as the leading authority in the field, he was waiting to speak on stage to a group of affluent dentists. How had things changed so much for Steve? His transition from a commoditized CPA to a recognized authority in his field began with a decision to play a game no one else knew was being played. He recognized that he was fighting an uphill battle in a crowded space and knew he had to do something to stand out from his competitors. He wanted to work smarter, not harder, and so he embraced the idea of authority marketing by publishing his first book.

Using his expertise and credentials, Steve was able to build his authority and leverage it to great success. He wrote several other short books, spoke at events, and used media appearances to showcase his knowledge and skills. And it paid off. Steve became a well-known expert in his field and was able to attract the exact type of clients he had always dreamed of attracting. And he was getting paid the fees that a few years ago would have seemed impossible to command.

As he waited backstage at the conference center, Steve couldn't help but feel grateful for the opportunity to speak to such a prestigious group of dentists. He knew that his message would be well received, and he was excited to share his expertise with the audience.

Finally, it was time for Steve to take the stage. He walked out to a packed room of dentists, all eager to hear what he had to say. Steve took a deep breath and began his presentation, confident in his ability to deliver a valuable and informative talk.

As he spoke, Steve could see the dentists hanging on his every word. They were engaged and interested in what he had to say, and Steve knew that he was making a real impact. When he finished his presentation, the room erupted in applause, and Steve knew that he had done his job well.

After his talk, Steve was approached by many of the dentists in attendance, all eager to learn more about his advanced tax planning strategies. Steve was happy to oblige, and he spent the rest of the conference answering questions and sharing his expertise with the attendees.

***

The single most valuable benefit to becoming an author is accelerating the Speed of Trust. When you do so you're not seen as someone who has something to sell, but instead as a thought leader that has something to teach. The key is to use authorship to establish trust before you ever sit down with someone. When you do this, you don't have to establish your credibility or make the case as to why you're the best resource. You can go right to discussing the problem and determining whether you are the right person to help. Your prospects are more willing to take your recommendations and agree to your fees without shopping around. In other words, authority reduces the sales cycle. Your prospects feel lucky to be talking to you and are going with you because of who you are rather than what you offer. This is because you have demonstrated in advance that you are a trustworthy expert.

Author=Author[ity]

The word "author" is part of the word "authority," and that connection is no coincidence. When you become an author, you are taking on a position of authority in your field. By writing a book, you are showcasing your expertise and establishing yourself as a thought leader in your industry. This not only sets you apart from your competition but also gives you the credibility and confidence to charge higher fees and attract the clients you want to work with. In short, becoming an author is a powerful way to build your authority and grow your business.

A Book Can Be Gifted

How many sales have you lost over the years after someone had a great conversation with you? You were confident they were going to buy, and then they came back and said, "I talked to so-and-so, and I don't think this is right for me now."

Here's what actually happened in that exchange:

Your prospect tried and failed to sell your service or offer to someone who didn't also watch that webinar, listen to that podcast, or consume the sales message. Because the "trusted advisor" wasn't there, they didn't "get it."
      The best part about a book is that it can do the talking for you, and it even does the talking for your prospect who needs to sell your ideas to their spouse or other trusted advisor.

You can see this in your own buying behavior. How many times have you told someone to check out a book that you enjoyed? I would bet that it's significantly more times than you have ever told someone to go check out a webinar that you've watched.

It is culturally normal behavior to share books. It is culturally abnormal and weird to share sales presentations, such as webinars or video sales letters. Many clients of mine report stories of their prospects sitting down and reading their book together with their spouse, and the couple coming up with the conclusion together to purchase my client's financial planning services. In highly competitive and skeptical niches like life insurance, the book can become a tool your prospects use to pass around and get outside opinions. While they're trying to make a buying decision, you're getting more and more exposure for free.

A well-written book is a tool that does all your selling for you. It's also a tool that has a history that people respect. Now tell me, are there any other sales tools quite like that?

In conclusion, writing a book can be a powerful and effective way for financial professionals to establish their credibility, showcase their expertise, and generate new business. The benefits of writing a book are clear, and the return on investment can be significant. With the right approach and the right support, it is possible to overcome the common challenges that many financial professionals face when writing a book. By following the steps outlined in this book and using the Short Book Formula, you too can write and publish a book that will help you stand out in a crowded market and attract more clients, bigger commissions, and higher fees.

Take action today and schedule a 15-minute phone call directly with me to discuss how we might be able to help you write your book. Go to www.theshortbookformula.com/schedule to access my online calendar link. Or, email me at paul@moreclientsmorefun.com Just mention that you are currently reading this book in your message.

Chapter 2

The Secret to Engaging Your Reader

When it comes to writing your book, there are key questions that you'll want to ask yourself to ensure the book's success. Some of these questions include:

1. What are my objectives for writing this book?
2. What do I want my readers to get out of it?
3. Who is my primary audience?
4. What pain is my audience experiencing because they haven't read my book yet?
5. What transformation will my audience experience once they read and implement the advice in my book?

When positioning his book for success, Mark Miller, CEO of Hilton Tax and Wealth Advisors, settled on several key points.

He wanted his book to introduce business owners to the value proposition of Hilton Tax and Wealth Advisors, introduce them to the concept of a Virtual Family Office, and give them reasons to see why their current CPA or tax preparer may not be giving them the best advice when it comes to reducing taxes.

Additionally, he wanted to give business owners hope and confidence that they can legally reduce their tax burden. His primary audience was business owners paying at least $20,000 in taxes per year. These business owners were experiencing frustration and dissatisfaction with their current tax advice, and Mark's book promised to provide them with the solutions they were seeking.

The success of Mark's book can be seen in the high close ratio of his initial appointments to new clients. By establishing his authority on the subject and providing a clear process, Mark is able to confidently discuss the benefits of his services without coming across as pushy.

Similar to my close ratio of 80% that I mentioned in an earlier chapter, Mark too is closing an amazing 80 percent. He attributes this success to the fact that every one of his prospects has read his book from cover to cover, giving them a deep understanding of his knowledge and the value, he brings to the table. This helps to rapidly build trust and credibility.

Unlock the Power of Emotional Connection

It's essential to understand the reader on a deeper level to ensure your content resonates with them. To do this, you must get inside their head and understand the thoughts they are having, as well as the emotions they are feeling. By understanding what is keeping them awake at night, what they are mad about, and their daily frustrations, you can create content that speaks directly to their needs. You can give them a sense of hope by letting them know that there is something out there that will help them reach their desired outcome. Content that speaks to these desires will form an emotional bond between the reader and your work. When done properly, it will have a lasting impact on the reader and be remembered long after they finish reading your material. It is only through this careful exploration of understanding their wants and needs can you truly connect with your readers.

Here are some questions to ask about your target ideal reader to help you come up with your hook for your book.

- What is keeping them awake at night?

- What are they mad about?

- What are their daily frustrations?

- What do they desire the most?

- What are they looking to achieve?

As you go through these questions, remember your ideal target reader wants to:

- Learn more about you/your business and how you can specifically help them.

- Get something they crave.

- Reduce pain, expenses, wasted time, etc.

- Gain pleasure, health, time, money, and comfort,

Insights Interviews

One of the best ways to answer the questions above with a high degree of certainty is to conduct what I call an "*Insights Interview*" with your ideal reader.

Michael Budnick, a financial advisor client of mine recently wrote and published his third book: *The Prosperous Nurse: Your Roadmap To Wealth, Health and Happiness.*

Michael had a number of nurse clients already, and he wanted to create a book that would magnetically attract more nurses to his financial planning services. So as part of his writing journey I gave him the assignment of conducting three insights interviews with his existing nurse clients.

Here were some of the insights he got directly back from one nurse named Michelle.

(Note, since these were existing clients, he framed the questions as "prior to us working together.")

Here are a few of the answers Michelle provided to his questions:

What are your pains?

I felt like I was on my own, with no personal guidance. I was one of 10,000 employees. I would get very little advice from the 403(b) representative at my hospital. I didn't feel like I had a personal connection to anyone, or that anyone was personally invested in my success. It was just me trying to figure out my finances on my own.

What are your frustrations?

There is little to no education for nurses about retirement. At the hospital where I work, we are lucky to have two choices for our retirement plans: a defined benefit or a defined contribution. However, I didn't even understand what those were. The education provided was not tailored to individuals and felt impersonal. There were only a few people at the hospital who were available to provide guidance, and it felt like there was no personal investment in my success. It was just a one-size-fits-all approach to retirement planning, with no consideration for my individual needs and circumstances.

What has kept you up at night?

The market has been volatile during the COVID-19 pandemic, and it feels like a roller coaster ride. I'm trying to stay positive and believe that everything will work out in the end, but it's hard not to worry about whether I will be okay in a few years. It's this uncertainty that keeps me up at night.

What do you want?

I want peace of mind in my life, including peace with my finances and relationships. I just want a peaceful existence overall.

What are your beliefs about money?

I believe it's important to have a savings account for unexpected expenses. I'm not a person who likes to leave things to chance and worry about things as they come up. I prefer to plan ahead and be conservative with my money. I know that at the end of the day, I'm the only one who can really help myself. Even though I have friends and people I can rely on, I try to be as self-sufficient as possible.

***

The key to effective insights interviews is to look for patterns. That's why I typically recommend doing a minimum of three insights interviews with your target reader. When you ask them the same questions, you'll start to see those patterns as well as the language they use to express themselves.

One interesting fact we discovered as a result of these insights interviews with nurses was that they didn't seem motivated to become rich. They were more motivated by security and overall quality of life.

Originally, we had planned to call Michael's book, "Smart Nurses Finish Rich," but because of this insight, we ended up changing the title (and all the content that flowed from it) to The Prosperous Nurse.

In conclusion, understanding your target ideal reader is essential to writing content that will resonate with them. To gain the necessary insight, it's helpful to conduct insights interviews with people who fit your target demographic. These conversations can help you discover their struggles and frustrations, their dreams and desires, as well as their motivations and goals. By connecting with them on an emotional level and speaking directly to their needs, you can create content that authentically engages readers. With the right approach and a genuine understanding of your reader's point of view, you can now craft content that instantly captures their attention and successfully converts readers into clients.

Chapter 3

The Short Book Formula

As a financial professional, you know how important the advice you give to your clients can be. It can literally help them with their financial success. As a result, there can be the temptation to want to pack in as much useful information into your book as possible. After all, this shows how well you know your subject matter, right?

However, sometimes a book that is too long and daunting can prevent your ideal clients from actually reading and benefiting from your expertise. I know this firsthand, having recently purchased a book by well-known CPA author Tom Wheelhouse, only to never make it past the first chapter.

In fact, research shows that only 9% of readers make it past the first chapter with longer business books. That's why The Short Book Formula focuses on creating a short, engaging book that will grab your clients' attention and provide them with valuable information upon which they can then immediately take action. Ideally, by hiring you to help them do so.

Here are nine methods we recommend to help ensure your readers not only buy your book, but they read it from cover to cover, thereby maximizing your chances of turning them into clients.

Keep It Short

For business books, shorter is often better than longer. Writing your book as concisely as possible can help ensure that essential information is communicated in a clear and impactful way. A short book allows readers to quickly digest the key points without being overwhelmed by hundreds of pages of text. The most valuable books are those that are well-structured, organized, and focused on providing actionable insights.

Here are a few examples of famous non-fiction books that adhered to this principle.

- *"The Art of War"* by Sun Tsu (96 pages)
- *"The Prince"* by Niccolo Machiavelli (94 pages)

- "*The Communist Manifesto*" by Karl Marx (40 pages)
- "*Animal Farm*" by George Orwell (58 pages)
- "*Go for No! Yes is the Destination, No is How You Get There*" by Richard Fenton (80 pages)
- "*The One-Minute Manager*" by Ken Blanchard (113 pages)

A short book also enables readers to more easily apply the content to their own unique situation. By limiting the length of the book, authors can focus directly on their target audience's needs and interests instead of rambling about topics that may not be relevant or useful. This helps ensure that readers receive maximum value from their investment in the book, allowing them to get started quickly with implementing strategies for success.

Remember, your prospective clients are busy people! They don't have time to read a 200-page novel masquerading as a business book. Stick to the essentials and make sure every word counts. We recommend 12,000 words.

Keep It Focused

When you're writing a shorter book, you can't afford to include fluff or filler content. Every sentence should serve a purpose and move the story forward.

It is important to choose one main topic or theme and focus on it. This will help keep the message focused and ensure that each sentence serves a purpose in furthering the ultimate end: them reaching out to you to do business.

As the person selling your thing, it's obvious that what you have is what your prospect needs. For prospects, however, it's not so simple. All potential buyers have a certain amount of fear about buying, which can manifest itself as doubt, trepidation, second-guessing, lack of self-confidence, foot dragging, irrational behavior, etc. Buyers doubt themselves because they've made bad choices in the past. They doubt your product or services because they don't understand it. Doubt is the natural state of a prospect. Accept it. Learn from it. Do something about it.

In my mind, the book is the most disarming, natural, and effective way to persuade someone into believing in themselves, your offer, and the future you can provide for them. Books are honest when written correctly. They are trustworthy by name alone. They are not a webinar or lead magnet or other "marketing trick" in prospects' minds. They are a
real thing—a value offer.

For us, a book is a powerful tool for belief change. When people's beliefs change, they carry a tremendous amount of momentum with them towards action. It manifests itself as excitement, commitment, and eagerness—the perfect set of buying behaviors.

If you have more topics than you want to cover, it is better to write multiple books than to try to cram everything into one book.

For example, my first book Smart Million Dollar Producer was narrowly focused on helping life insurance agents tap into both the power of LinkedIn as well as my then-business partner's coaching program for them.

My second book, Million Dollar Producer, dropped the tie-in with my former business partner and instead focused specifically on the secret sauce I provided financial professionals to tap into LinkedIn to land high-value clients.

This third book is now narrowly focused on helping financial professionals write and publish a book within 6 weeks.

Bottom line: The more focused the intended reader and the subject matter, the easier it is to attract your ideal reader to want to read your book. Second, to actually get them to read it. And third, as a result of the previous two actions, motivate them to then reach out to you for help.

Use Client Stories and Case Studies To Make It Compelling

To drive the message home, it is useful to include specific client examples and case studies which will help readers understand the concepts more clearly. These examples and case studies provide vivid descriptions and detailed facts, giving readers an emotional connection with what they are reading. Using these types of resources can help create a captivating story that resonates with readers on a personal level, as they can relate their own experiences to what they have read. Furthermore, using words with higher semantic richness allows authors to create stories that go beyond the obvious surface-level information. This will help further engage readers, immersing them in a unique narrative experience which has the power to make lasting impressions. All of these techniques combined can contribute towards developing truly inspiring pieces of writing that offer deep insights into broad topics or themes.

What if I can't use actual client names in a case study?

That's perfectly okay. One thing I recommend you do is simply change the name and tell the story, or even create a composite story of a few of your clients that highlight the results that you have helped them achieve.

Write for People Who Believe What You Believe

We don't trust everyone. We trust people within our community. Every decision we make in our lives is a piece of communication. It's our way of saying something about who we are and what we believe. This is why authenticity matters. This is why you have to say and do the things you actually believe. Because the things you say and do are symbols of who you are. And we look for those symbols so we can find people who believe what we believe. So if you're putting out false symbols, you will attract people to those symbols but you won't be able to form trust with them.

If you write about what you believe, you will attract people who believe what you believe. This is how you magnetically attract your ideal clients to want to reach out to you as a result of reading your book. People want to do business with those who they feel they can legitimately trust.

Make it Multimedia

Video is an incredibly effective way to establish "know, like, and trust" with a complete stranger. It allows the viewer to see and hear the person they are interested in forming a relationship with. Seeing someone's facial expressions and body language can quickly form an emotional connection that might take much longer to form over text. It also serves as a personal touchpoint, allowing potential clients to feel as if they know the person on the other side of the screen.

One way we do this with our clients in our Million Dollar Producer Author Program is to conduct an "author interview" on video with our client that we then include in their book as well as use in their other marketing to help promote the book.

Here is one such example.

Larry Evans is an experienced CPA who specializes in advanced tax planning for the ultra-affluent. We recently helped him publish his new book: *The Billionaire Tax Solution: How To Legally Pay ZERO Taxes Like The Ultra-Affluent.*

Please do not contact Larry directly. He is busy with his businesses and personal life. His comments here speak for

themselves and were generously given without compensation of any kind.

Here is the link to the 15-minute author interview we did that you can watch as an example if you'd like.

http://www.theshortbookformula.com/resource

Publish it to Amazon

Publishing your book to Amazon is a great way to get your book out into the world without having to go through the traditional publishing route. By using Amazon, you can make your book available to potential readers quickly and easily. Not only does this make it easier for interested prospects to purchase and receive a physical hard copy of your work, but it also eliminates the need to deal with agents and publishers who may not be interested in publishing your work.

    I can publish a book like the one you are reading now for you on Amazon within a few days - once you have the manuscript and book cover ready. Not only does Amazon allow you to print a single physical book on demand, but by using Amazon Prime you can ship this book anywhere in the United States at no additional charge. This is revolutionary!

Be Clear From The Beginning About Your Intentions

Let the reader know from the beginning that this is an introduction to your services and a conversation starter. And that's why you wrote the book. Do not shy away from stating this!

You may recall from the beginning of this book how I did that. In the chapter called "My Promise To You" I wrote:

"This book exists for two reasons:

Reason #1: So that you'll eventually hire me and my team to help
you implement everything you read here.

Reason #2: To inspire and motivate you on the benefits of writing and publishing a short book so that you'll actually want to do Reason #1 as quickly as possible."

Nobody likes "bait and switch." So, by being upfront with your reader about your goals for the book and what they can expect to get out of it.

Make it direct-response

Direct response describes a form of marketing that is designed to get a response from the recipient. Unlike most marketing, which is typically one-way in the direction, direct response marketing is meant as a two-way "conversation" between the sender and the recipient. Your goal as an author should be to engage with your reader and inspire them to take action. The Short Book Formula is all about getting your readers to take the actions you prescribe. You'll notice that throughout this book I use call-to-action (CTAs) where I deem appropriate.

Don't go it alone

Working with an experienced guide such as my company can be incredibly beneficial for those looking to write and publish their book in as little as six weeks. With us, you will receive personalized attention and guidance to ensure that the book is in your voice, that it resonates with your ideal reader, and most importantly, gives you a positive return on investment. We understand what it takes to create a successful narrative guaranteed to capture the attention of readers. Furthermore, our marketing services help ensure that your message is spread far and wide so you can start experiencing the rewards of your hard work as soon as possible.

Our Million Dollar Producer Author Program is designed to help you go from start to finish in writing and publishing your book in as little as six weeks.

***

Now that you've learned the steps to creating a powerful and impactful book in just six weeks, it's time to get started! Crafting a book quickly may seem like an insurmountable task at first, but with our support, it's very doable. The key is crafting content that is succinct yet effective. Additionally, creating direct-response calls-to-action for your reader to reach out to you to engage in your services will help turn your book into a rich source of leads, appointments, and revenue with your ideal clients. Get ready to jumpstart your creative process and take the next step towards becoming a successful published author!

Go to: www.theshortbookformula.com/schedule to schedule a complimentary 15-minute consultation to see if our services are right for you.

Chapter 4

Short Book Formula Examples

At this point, I thought it would be helpful to show you several real-world book examples that I've had the privilege to assist with and publish for my clients. Each of these books are written by everyday financial professionals who understand the power of packaging their knowledge, experience, and insights into a short book to create their desired marketing and sales goals.

These books are all under 100 pages and focused on a specific, big idea that resonates with a targeted reader. They are easy to read in just an hour or so, making them a more efficient and effective way to share one's knowledge and expertise. In contrast to traditional 200-page books that can be time-consuming to read and write, short books offer a powerful alternative that drive real world revenue results.

Title: *The Due Diligence Project*
Subtitle: *How Open-Source, Peer-Reviewed Due Diligence is Supercharging Elite CPA Firms and Family Offices, While Disrupting a Multi-Trillion Dollar Industry*
Author: *Alex Sonkin*

Title: *The Prosperous Nurse*
Subtitle: *Your Roadmap To Wealth, Health, and Happiness*
Author: *Michael Budnick*

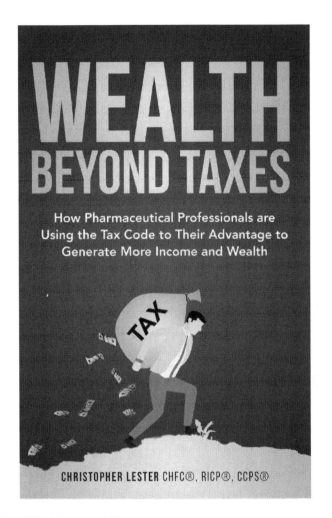

Title: *Wealth Beyond Taxes*
Subtitle: *How Pharmaceutical Professionals are Using the Tax Code to Their Advantage to Generate More Income and Wealth.*
Author: *Christopher Lester*

Title: *The Tax Savvy Real Estate Professional*
Subtitle: *Proactive Tax Planning For Maximum Earnings and Savings*
Author: *Danny Fink*

Title: *The ESG Data Revolution*
Subtitle: *Sustainable Fuel For Tomorrow's Business*
Author: Michael Poisson

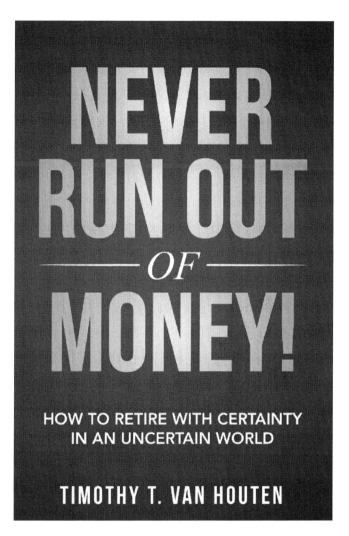

Title: *Never Run Out of Money!*
Subtitle: *How To Retire With Certainty In An Uncertain World*
Author: *Timothy T. Van Houten*

Title: *In Search Of The Perfect Investment*
Subtitle: *Redefining Wealth and Retirement Income Strategies*
Author: Robert Padilla

Title: *The Tax-Free Business Owner*
Subtitle: *How Business Owners Can Use The Tax Code To Legally Pay ZERO TAXES*
Author: *Mark Miller*

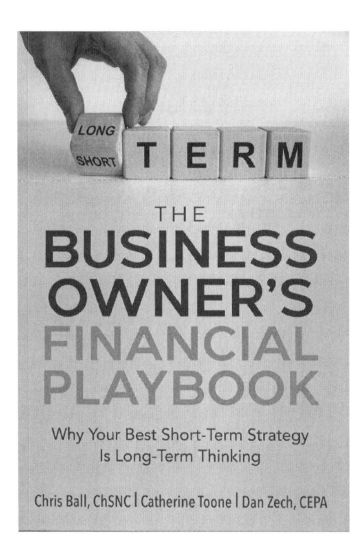

Title: *The Business Owner's Financial Playbook*
Subtitle: *Why Your Best Short-Term Strategy Is Long-Term Thinking*
Authors: *Chris Ball, Catherine Toone, and Dan Zech*

In this final example, you'll notice that there are three authors. This is a great way to collaboratively create a book that business partners can all derive maximum value from and can become a go-to piece of marketing collateral for the firm.

Chapter 5

Your Book As Your Business Card

As of the time I am writing this, you can purchase a single copy of your book from Amazon for roughly $3.50 plus tax. If you have Amazon Prime you can then send a copy of the book anywhere in the United States at no additional cost, and it will arrive in roughly 2-3 business days.

Conversely, if you meet with a lot of people in person you can order a larger quantity of books directly from Amazon for less than $2.50 per book.

Either way, once you have your book, you should start thinking about maximizing it as your new business card as the way Jane did to great success!

"The Secret to Networking Success: How Jane Used Her Book to Stand Out and Attract New Clients"

*The following is a fictitious story based on a composite of real client feedback we have received about the dramatic difference their books have made for them.

The networking event at the local Chamber of Commerce was packed with people, all jostling for attention and trying to make connections. Jane stood awkwardly on the edge of the room, feeling out of place and overwhelmed. She hated these types of events. The forced small talk and awkward pitches always left her feeling drained and unfulfilled.

But this time was different. This time, she had a secret weapon - her new book. As a financial advisor, Jane had spent years honing her skills and knowledge, and she wanted to share that expertise with the world. So she had written a book on personal finance, filled with practical tips and strategies for anyone looking to improve their financial situation.

As she clutched her purse, filled with 20 copies of her new book, she took a deep breath and tried to push aside her nerves. She had to do this - she had to make connections and grow her business. So, she squared her shoulders and stepped into the fray.

At first, it was tough going. People were rushing past her, barely giving her a second glance. But as she approached each person with a friendly smile and a copy of her book, she could see their attitudes shift. They stopped, engaged in conversation, and listened as she asked them thoughtful questions to learn more about who they were and vice versa.

"Here, I wrote this book on personal finance," Jane said as she handed a copy to a young couple. "I think you might find it helpful."

The couple eagerly accepted the book and thanked Jane for her generosity. As they continued to talk, Jane could see their eyes light up as they asked her questions about her work and expertise.

"You know, I'm actually looking for a financial advisor," the husband said. "I think you might be exactly what we're looking for. Could we set up a meeting to discuss things further?"

Over the course of the evening, Jane handed out 20 copies of her book and immediately received seven requests for appointments from those whom she engaged in conversation. As she drove home that night, tears of joy streamed down her face. She couldn't believe the difference a book had made. It had given her the confidence and authority she needed to stand out in a crowded room and make meaningful connections. And now she had a whole new group of prospective clients eager to engage with her.

From that point on, Jane was a changed woman. No longer did she dread networking events - in fact, she couldn't wait to attend as many as she possibly could. She had discovered the power of her book to attract new clients and she was eager to continue leveraging that power to grow her business.

At each event, she followed the same strategy - she struck up conversations with potential clients, asked them thoughtful questions about their lives and careers, and for those who seemed genuinely interested in Jane's book and expertise she would offer them a complimentary copy and schedule an appointment.

For those who accepted her book as a gift, she would gently ask them to spend an hour in advance of their appointment to read it. That way they could both make the best use of their time when they met in person or on Zoom.

"*I can't believe how well this is working,*" Jane marveled to a friend. "*I used to hate networking events, but now I'm having so much fun.*"

As Jane's business continued to grow, she found herself with a full schedule of appointments with new clients. And at each meeting, she made a point to ask for a referral and offer a copy of her book.

To her surprise, she found that her prospects were more than happy to oblige. Even though she was only asking for one referral, they would often give her a list of two or three people who they thought could benefit from her services. And they were excited to make the referral, eager to share their positive experience they had with Jane with their friends and colleagues.

"*I can't believe how easy this is,*" Jane thought to herself as she jotted down the names of her new referral prospects. "*I used to struggle to get even one referral, and now people are practically throwing them at me.*"

As she thought about her conversations with her new clients, Jane realized that part of the reason for this sudden influx of referrals was their perception of her as a quasi-celebrity. As an author, she had a level of prestige and authority that set her apart from other financial advisors. And her clients were proud to be associated with her, eager to share their relationship with others. And sometimes they even asked her to autograph their copy of her book!

Chapter 6

The Value of a Book Launch Party

According to a study by MarketingSherpa, it is 50% easier to sell to an existing customer than it is to acquire a new one. This means that by focusing on your existing client base, you can generate new business more efficiently and with less effort. In addition, existing customers are also more likely to spend more and be more loyal, leading to increased revenue and long-term growth for your business.

That's why having a "book launch party" with your existing clients, vendors, and strategic partners can be a valuable and effective way to promote your book. A book launch party is a celebration of your book's release, and can provide an opportunity to share your book with a group of supportive and interested individuals.

Another benefit of a book launch party is that it can help build buzz and excitement around your book. A book launch party can be a fun and engaging event, and can generate positive word-of-mouth and social media buzz. You could even contact your local newspaper and invite them to your party and request they do a story on it.

A book launch party can be held in person or online, depending on your preferences and the circumstances. An in-person book launch party can provide an opportunity for face-to-face networking and engagement, while an online book launch party can reach a wider audience and be more easily accessible.

Client Case Files: "Maximizing Your Network: How Jake Barton Used His Book Launch Party to Attract Over $130,000 in New Business"

Introduction:

In this case study, we'll explore how our client Jake. was able to use his book launch party to promote his financial planning business and attract new clients.

Background:

Jake is a holistic financial planner and has just released a book with our help on the topic of comprehensive financial planning for healthcare professionals. He was looking for ways to promote the book and his financial planning business. He decided to host a book launch party to celebrate the release of his book and share it with his network.

Objectives:

Promote Jake's financial planning business and attract new clients
Share Jake's expertise and knowledge with others through the book
Engage with Jake's existing clients to create an opportunity for them to become interested in additional services

Strategy:

Jake invited his existing clients, as well as other professionals in the healthcare industry, to the book launch party. He held the event at a local venue and provided refreshments and snacks. During the event, Jake presented a short presentation about his book and led a Q&A session where guests could ask questions. He also invited the local newspaper to attend, which they did. He offered each guest three complimentary copies of his book. One copy was signed and that was meant for them to keep. The other two copies were given with explicit instructions that they should be given to like-minded colleagues, family members, or friends.

Results:

The book launch party was a success, with a high attendance rate and positive feedback from guests. As a result of the event, six of his existing clients asked to schedule appointments so they could discuss additional services that were now top of mind, eight of the other attendees (who were not yet clients) decided to schedule time with Jake to discuss his services, and lastly Jake was able to attract eleven new referrals. The cost to Jake for holding the event was less than $1,000. Three months later when I spoke to him, Jake calculated that he earned an additional $130,000 worth of business as a direct result of the event that was only made possible because he wrote and published his book.

Conclusion:

Hosting a book launch party can be a valuable and effective way to promote your business and attract new clients. By sharing your expertise and knowledge through a book, you can engage with your existing network and build buzz around your business. Jake's success demonstrates the impact that a book launch party can have on driving business growth and success. Jake is already planning his next book and wants to have it launched in 2023.

Chapter 7

How To Grow A 7-Figure Financial Practice

Guest Chapter by Tony Maree Torrey, LA's Foremost Business Success Coach and Author of Your Million Dollar Accelerator - 6 Proven Strategies to Grow a 7-Figure Financial Practice.

For 20 years, Financial Professionals and Founding CEOs (often the same person) have hired me to help them scale their businesses. I've had the good fortune to work with some very high-level producers and those who just needed a helping hand and some smart strategies to play at that level.

I was excited when Paul invited me to contribute to this book because I've been working closely with him since 2014. Paul has been both my client and colleague, and it's been an honor to help him grow his business to seven figures. Hopefully, I can do my part here to help you grow your business to seven figures too.

Once you work with Paul to set up your author-ity and get your book published, the next question likely on your mind is, now what?

How do I turn this into new revenue for my business without burning myself out in the process?

The sad truth is that too many financial professionals hit an income ceiling, and never make the kind of money (or the kind of impact) that they deserve. In my experience, there are three core questions that need to be answered for you to build a 7-figure practice.

1. **Attract:** How do I generate awareness about my book and, by extension, my services, thereby attracting my ideal target prospects?

2. **Convert:** How do I influence these readers to not just acquire a copy of my book, but to read it, absorbing its core message?
3. **Accelerate:** How do I stay top-of-mind, positioning myself as their first choice when they're ready to move forward into getting professional support?

You want to build fast, simple, ethical, and persuasive systems that you can leverage in a myriad of ways to stay top of mind until the timing is right for your prospects to reach out. Importantly, scaling up should never compromise your well-being. True success lies in optimizing processes, ultimately liberating your time.

'Now' vs. 'Future' Buyers

According to an extensive survey conducted by marketing guru Dean Jackson, over a two-year period:

- 50% of people who inquire about a service, never buy anything from anybody.

That's just life.

So, we've got the 50% left that we can potentially work with, and of that 50%

- 15% are what we call "now buyers." They're going to do something with someone in the next 90 days.

Obviously, we want the Now Buyers to work with YOU when they are ready to purchase.

- 85% of these remaining buyers are "Future Buyers" and they're looking to purchase between 90 days and two years.

So, our job is to make it easy for the Now Buyers to raise their hands and identify themselves to us. AND for us to set up the Future Buyers so that when they're ready, they'll think of you and put time on your calendar rather than someone else's.

Attracting Your Perfect Future Clients

Hitting that 7-figure mark in the financial realm is all about precision. It's not about casting a wide net but zeroing in on the elite few who truly value what you offer. This isn't necessarily about volume; it's about quality. It's about connecting with those who see your vision, value and want to be a part of it. To become the go-to for these high-caliber clients, here's the strategy to consider:

Amplify with Podcasts: The 1:Many Strategy in Action

Podcasts have shifted from the sidelines to the spotlight, becoming the go-to platform for deep dives and candid conversations. Think of it as a coffee chat, but broadcasted for an audience hungry for insights. And when you've written a book? That's like adding a dash of credibility to your coffee. It's not just about expertise; it's about having a story that resonates. With your book as a testament to your knowledge, podcast hosts will see you as a valuable voice to bring to the table. And because it's usually just a simple conversation, it works well even if you're speaking skills feel rusty.

Webinars & LinkedIn: The 1:Many Power Play

Webinars are gold mines for showcasing expertise, while LinkedIn is the stage where professionals gather. Combine the two, and you've got a dynamite strategy to amplify your book's message.

Here's the playbook:

1. Pick Your Topic: Align with your book's core message.
2. Build Buzz on LinkedIn: Launch a LinkedIn event, invite connections, and get them talking.
3. Maximize Reach Post-Event: Record the webinar. Share it. Pair it with resources to keep the momentum going. Leverage sound bites and repurpose, repurpose, repurpose!

Picture yourself in Brandon's shoes. He's a financial advisor, fresh off completing his short book on tax-saving strategies. Brandon is eager to put it to work attracting his perfect future clients. The ink is barely dry, and he's buzzing with excitement. The next challenge: to get this invaluable tool into the right hands. The solution? A webinar, amplified through LinkedIn. After his session on tax-saving techniques, Brandon had:

- 285 people sign up
- 76 live attendees
- Three appointments booked on his calendar

And best of all, these were all prospects who valued his expertise because they attended his webinar, and were now excited to speak with him further about their own unique situations.

Additionally, Brandon was able to get his book into the hands of all 285 people who registered, add everyone to his email list, and continue to engage with them and grow their relationship on and off LinkedIn.

Best of all, we set the webinar up to be evergreen, turning it into a client attraction machine that could be used over and over, freeing up Brandon's time.

Seminars & Books: A Dynamic Duo for Lasting Impact

In-person seminars are magic. It's where you lock eyes with your audience, share your wisdom, and create those unforgettable moments. But what if you could make that magic last even after the curtains close?

Here's how to make your talk unforgettable:

1. Blend Seminar & Book: As you craft your seminar, sprinkle in golden nuggets from your book. It's like giving them a movie trailer; they'll be itching to dive into the full story.

2. Gift Your Legacy: As the seminar wraps up, surprise them. Hand out copies of your book. It's not just a book; it's a piece of you, a token of gratitude. And as they flip through its pages, they're bound to relive the seminar magic and resonate with your expertise.

"Books as Engagement Boosters: A Winning Strategy"

Several of my clients have unlocked a brilliant strategy. During their seminars, they use their book as a coveted prize for audience members who nail an answer. But the genius doesn't stop there. They promise a copy of their book for those who schedule an appointment. This tactic does wonders: it not only keeps the audience on their toes during the talk but also fuels excitement. The cherry on top? Those appointment no-shows? They've plummeted. The anticipation of receiving the book keeps attendees committed and eager for their one-on-one time.

3. Start Local, Dream Global: Kick things off in your backyard. Perfect your seminar, gather rave reviews, and then? Spread your wings. With each success, aim bigger. Collaborate with industry giants, target grander venues, and watch as your influence grows.

With seminars as your stage and your book as the encore, you're not just sharing knowledge; you're creating an experience, a legacy. And as attendees share their experiences and your book, you're not just an expert; you're a legend in the making.

Your Book's Digital Home: Engage, Capture, Connect

In a world where everyone's online, your book needs its own digital spotlight. It's not just about being seen; it's about creating a magnetic pull that draws readers in and keeps them engaged. A book-focused website isn't just a page; it's your book's home, a place where readers can dive deeper, connect with you, and be part of your journey. Amazon and other platforms? Great for visibility. But for that personal touch, that direct connection with your readers? You need a space that's uniquely yours. Here's how to make your book's digital home a powerhouse:

1. Craft a Book-Centric Site: Think of your website as your book's extended cover. It should scream the essence of your book. Dive into the core themes, flaunt those rave reviews, introduce yourself, and give them a taste of the magic inside.

2. Offer an Audiobook Twist: We live in a multitasking world. Some read, some listen. Why not cater to both? An audiobook version means your wisdom can be absorbed anytime, anywhere—whether they're jogging, cooking, or just relaxing.

3. Entice with Value: Want their details? Give them something they can't resist. How about a free audiobook version for those who sign up? It's a win-win. They get value, and you get a direct line to engage, nurture, and build lasting relationships.

With a dedicated book website, you're not just another author. You're a brand, a thought leader, and a go-to expert in your field.

Turbocharge Your Growth: Email Marketing Meets Book Wisdom

In the financial world, 'acceleration' isn't just about speed. It's about hitting those goals with precision and flair. And while the digital age has thrown a ton of tools our way, there's one oldie but goldie that still packs a punch: email marketing.

Why? Emails aren't just fleeting notifications; they're personal invitations. They don't just pop up and vanish; they sit in an inbox, patiently waiting for that click. And the best part? They're speaking to an audience that's already tuned in, folks who've said, "Yes, I want to hear from you."

Now, let's add some spice to this mix: your book. Pairing email marketing with the gems from your book? That's like adding rocket fuel. Share a snippet, a case study, a teaser, and watch as you not only establish your expertise but also build a bond based on trust and value.

But it doesn't stop at just sharing. Craft your emails like a story, guiding your readers from curiosity to that "Aha!" moment, and then to action. With strategic calls-to-action, aligned with your book's essence, you can smoothly lead them to your online calendar. The result? A chat, a connection, and a potential game-changer for both you and them.

In Conclusion: A 7-Figure Vision

Building a 7-figure financial practice is no small feat. It requires vision, tenacity, and the effective harnessing of various strategies to achieve your desired goals. With Paul G. McManus's insight on authorship as your foundation, this chapter has equipped you with potent tactics to Attract, Convert, and Accelerate growth, helping you morph from being just a financial professional to a thriving authority in your field.

Strategies such as speaking on podcasts and hosting webinars via LinkedIn are powerful in garnering visibility and attracting your ideal prospects. The integration of your book into in-person seminars not only cements your authority but also fosters a lasting engagement with your audience. Meanwhile, a book-centered website serves as a one-stop hub for interested readers, enabling you to capture leads and nurture relationships.

Finally, strategic email marketing, when fused with your book, can catalyze acceleration in your business growth, transforming subscribers into clients when they're ready to take that step.

The Art and Science of Achieving Seven Figures

Consistently hitting a million dollars or more takes focus and knowledgeable support in building the proven systems designed to get you there. I invite you to explore these methods in greater detail by visiting my book's website at:
www.yourmilliondollaraccelerator.com

If you prefer a direct conversation, you can reach out to me at tonymaree@tonymaree.com. Mention that you're reading this chapter in your email, and I'll have a special gift ready for you.

Here's to your future success!

PART 3

THE PATH FORWARD

Chapter 8

The Next Step

Congratulations! You are on the verge of achieving a major milestone in your career: becoming a published author. With your book, you can attract more of your ideal target clients and stand out in a crowded marketplace.

Just imagine the pride you'll feel as you hold your book in your hands and show it off to your loved ones, clients, and future prospects. And the satisfaction of having someone you've never met start a phone call with the words, *"I read your book and want to work with you."* Trust me, it's an incredibly fulfilling feeling that makes all the work of writing and publishing a book completely worth it.

To have a successful financial practice, it's essential to understand what your clients want and deliver it. Your book can be a powerful tool in this regard – it becomes your "salesperson in print," showcasing what you have to offer and speaking directly to your ideal clients. A well-written book is a tool that does all your selling for you. It's also a tool that has a history that people respect.

Don't Hesitate. The Time Is Now!

I wrote this book for two primary reasons: 1) to help inspire and motivate financial professionals like you on the benefits of writing and publishing a short book, and 2) to extend an invitation to see if working together makes sense - for both of us.

If you like what you have read so far let me ask you to consider these three questions:

1. Would you like to have the recognition and status that comes with being a published author?
2. Are you an experienced financial professional who truly brings value to your clients, and would love the opportunity to work with more ideal clients?
3. Do you value working with an expert to guide you, bring out the best in you and prevent mistakes?

If your answers are three yeses, then as I see it, you have two pathways in front of you at this very moment in time.

1. You can close this book and do nothing with the information I shared. (If you've made it this far, I surely hope this is not an option.)
2. You can schedule a 15–30-minute Zoom call with me to ask me any questions you have about our program and determine if it's a good fit. You can schedule your call on my calendar using the following link: www.theshortbookformula.com/schedule There's absolutely no fee, no obligation, no risk, and nothing to lose by scheduling this call with me.

I understand your goals are uniquely yours. This call is all about helping you decide if enrolling in our Million Dollar Producer Author Program will help you achieve the specific goals you have in mind and whether it is a good fit for both of us.

Why I'm Uniquely Qualified To Help You

I'm a firm believer that you are uniquely qualified to be working with certain people – not everybody but people who "get" you and what you and your business stand for.

I feel the same about my business, and in order for us to see if we are a good fit, I'd like to take a moment now to share a bit more about myself and my background.

To that end I had my colleague, Tony Maree Torrey, LA's Foremost Success Coach, interview me so you can get to know me better and make a judgment for yourself to see if you think I might be the right person to help you.

The recorded video is 18 min. long

www.theshortbookformula.com/video

I look forward to hearing from you, and more importantly, working together to help you become a published author so you can attract your ideal clients.

Resources

Throughout *The Short Book Formula*, I have shared a number of suggested resources. To help you with the most up-to-date list of these resources, I decided to create a private, reader-only web page where you can see all my recommended resources.

By putting these on a web page instead of inside this book, it will allow me to make changes and include new resources as I find them.

www.theshortbookformula.com/resource

About Paul G. McManus

Paul G. McManus is the Founder of More Clients More Fun LLC, MCMF Publishing, Creator of The Million Dollar Producer LinkedIn Program, and Host of The Million Dollar Producer Show Podcast. He has worked closely with over 500+ financial advisors, CPAs, life insurance producers, and business advisors since 2015. He is also the author of *Million Dollar Producer: The Secret Playbook For Financial Professionals To Land High-Value Clients Using LinkedIn*. He lives in San Diego, California with his wife Atsuko and his two Boston Terriers, Moo and Potato Chips. You can contact him directly at paul@moreclientsmorefun.com

DON'T FORGET THIS!

Get My Free 1-Hour Training

How To Use A Short Book To Generate 30+ Warm Leads From LinkedIn Per Month

When sorted by income 60% of LinkedIn users in the United States have an income of $100,000+.

41 percent of millionaires are on LinkedIn.

More than any other social network out there, the average user on LinkedIn is affluent. And where there's money, there are opportunities.

And as an exclusive and special gift for readers of *The Short Book Formula*, you'll get free access to this complementary must-have 1-hour video training.

Go to **www.theshortbookformula.com/bonus** to claim.

Made in the USA
Monee, IL
30 April 2024